The Voice of the Quiet Ones

C000269202

Reflections on an introvert's life

An Essay/Memoir
By
Mary Lunnen

Be you x
Mary Lunnen

Other Publications

Flying in the Face of Fear – Surviving Cervical Cancer 1998 (out of print but available online)

Dare to Blossom – Coaching and Creativity 2008

Dare to Blossom Rediscovery Cards 2013 (only available direct from Mary)

The Dare to Blossom Rediscovery Cards Companion Guide 2016

Mary has been a contributing author to several other books, including three volumes of the 365 Series.

She was also commissioned to write *Cervical Cancer – The Essential Guide* 2010, with an updated edition in 2018, by need2know books.

Inspiration

The name 'Dare to Blossom' was inspired by this quote, which still sits on a card I bought years ago, rather faded now, pinned to the cork board next to my desk as I write.

"...and then the day came when the risk to remain tight in a bud was more painful than the risk it took to blossom."

[It is usually attributed to Anais Nin, recently I learned that the true author was Elizabeth Appell. You can find the information for yourself through an Internet search.]

Dedication

This book is dedicated to everyone who has brought me to this point in my life today, with deep gratitude. If you read this, you will know the vital part you have played.

To my sister, Sue Jarvis, for being the family historian who has discovered all kinds of connections that were previously unknown to us. And for being there for me to discuss memories of our childhood, now we are 'the older generation'. Most of all, simply for being you.

To my husband Dave for also being simply you, and for helping me realise that it is OK for me to do the same.

Preface

Welcome, welcome to this reflection upon my journey to the realisation that I am one of the quiet ones.

And then to discover that there is nothing 'wrong' about preferring to be quiet. To learn about the qualities of introversion and how those have equal value in the world to the qualities of our extrovert fellow humans.

All of us are at different points on a scale of introversion to extroversion. A scale that is yet another of those differences in the ways our brains work. Differences that are being recognised under the banner of 'neuro-diversity'. A diversity to be celebrated along with all others. A diversity that brings so many gifts to the human race and to our world as they are beginning to be recognised and valued.

For so many centuries, anyone different was seen as 'abnormal', or 'wrong'. Now we begin to see those qualities as simply different.

This book grew from several sources. The first is the writing I have been creating for over two years, working on a book to take readers through the Compass Rose coaching process.

In the early drafts I included memoir sections, which seemed appropriate to begin with, and yet as time went on, they didn't seem to work within the book. The title that has emerged for that book at present is "The Power of Your Compass Rose." (with a sub-title still evolving).

Later, I was interviewed by Siobhan A. Riordan for Silver Tent TV, and she suggested a second conversation to explore my power as a 'quiet one'. I think it was Francesca Cassini, founder of the Silver Tent (a community for women over fifty) who gave that interview the title "The Powerful Voice of the Quiet Ones".

After that, in connection with my short talk of the same title at the HerStory

Conference in Wellington, New Zealand, I asked to write a chapter for the HerStory Anthology Series. That volume includes four others from speakers at the first HerStory Wellington Conference held on 28th and 29th November 2019.

I am very grateful to Getrude Matshe, the woman who has created the vision of the HerStory movement – hundreds of conferences in locations around the world, with thousands of women, and men, sharing their stories. Witnessing each other's stories is inspiring, healing and empowering. Truly an example of the power of 'Together we rise.'

In relation to the writing for "The Power of Your Compass Rose", once I had booked the trip to New Zealand, to attend the conference, and to visit my sister and her family in the South Island, near Christchurch, things began to shift.

I knew that, in addition to the excitement of travelling and meeting new people at the conference, and as well as the joy of reconnecting with my sister and all her family after many years – there was another element.

That journey was a spiritual odyssey, there was something that needed to emerge to add to the book. At the time of writing, this is still germinating, the first part is this book.

A note on the sub-title: "Reflections on an introvert's life." People say to me: "You can't possibly be an introvert, when you give talks and travel the world."

As I discuss in more detail in these pages, there are as many variations of 'an introvert' as there are people, each of us is different. Being an introvert doesn't necessarily mean you are shy, although I was when I was younger. For me, it means I need quiet time to recharge my energy, and maybe that I need to feel safe before I step out, before I step up, into my power.

Over the years I have discovered ways of doing this. A support network is one. Being grounded in myself, in my peace within, is another. Mixed in with this story, with my memories, you will find more tools and techniques. Maybe some of those will be the nuggets that you take away from reading this book

Mary Lunnen, February 2020

The Beginning

When I was born, I am sure I had what people used to call 'a good pair of lungs,' which I would have used powerfully to make my needs known.

Aged about six months

Later, as a young girl growing up in the 1950s, I was brought up to be 'quiet'. I suppose most children were at that time. We were taught not to make noise, not to upset Daddy. I was frightened during a lot of my childhood. Raised voices terrified me, especially angry ones. Especially male voices.

I later learned that my father was physically violent towards my mother, before I was born. She told me, and I can only take on trust that this was so, that she had to protect me as an unborn child by curling up and taking his beatings on her back. If it is true that the developing foetus is influenced by the experiences of the mother, that could be another reason for my fear.

My sister and I both remember our mother mentioned one, or maybe two miscarriages before I was born, which she told us were caused by our father.

This makes me sad, yet I am not judging my father for this. In those days it was 'normal', and the fact that it is no longer so, at least amongst my community, is something to celebrate, even if there is much more to be achieved.

My father was not violent towards me, (or to my sister and brother as far as I know), apart from the occasional spanking when I was naughty, also normal in those times. I remember him playing games with us and telling us stories.

My mother and father met when they were both stationed in Plymouth during the second World War. They had each already experienced tragedy. My mother had nursed her mother, my grandmother, as she died, after a series of strokes.

When my sister was researching our family history, after our mother had gone, she obtained a copy of our grandmother's death certificate, which gave the cause of death as cervical cancer. We will never know if our mother knew about this, in those times, family, and even the patient themselves, were often not told about a cancer diagnosis. This very poignant to me as I too experienced that disease.

My maternal grandmother Ethel Clayton

Just before my parents married, my mother had been told that the man she was in love with was missing in action presumed dead. (He did in fact return safely and contacted her later, but by then she was married.)

My mother was born in1921 in Karachi, which was then in India, now in Pakistan, while her father was running his business from there. Her family came from Yorkshire, and they returned there when she was around six or seven. Her father died not long after that.

The photo below is of my mother in her ATS (Army Territorial Service) uniform, around the time she met my father.

My mother, Joan Nunn

My father was born in 1915 in Essex. During the First World War, while he was still very young, he was sent away for safety to stay with a family in the country.

I am told that they wrote to his mother asking if they could adopt him. She arrived unannounced and took him away. At that age he would not have remembered who she was so it must have been a severe shock for him.

My mother and father, soon after they married

My father had been engaged to an American woman and was all set to join her there just before the Second World

War, when he was told she had died in a train crash. Given all that, and the uncertainties of war time, no wonder he and my mother married quickly as so many people did at that time.

It was also a time when people tended to stay together literally for better and for worse, through everything that life threw at them. Often, in those well-used words 'for the sake of the children'.

There is no way of knowing how different my life, and that of my sister and my brother, would have been if our mother and father had chosen differently.

My personal experience has been that I have forgiven the events of the past, even as I acknowledge the effects they have had on me and others in my family.

Some thoughts on power

Reflecting on early experiences of power, it is not surprising many of us choose to remain silent, to keep ourselves safe in the best way we can, by being unseen as much as possible. By hiding, and not standing out. By suppressing our power, disowning it entirely.

I am fortunate not to have experienced any severe physical violence directed at me in my life, though I did experience plenty of emotional, controlling behaviour. I am mentioning this not because I feel sorry for myself, or to ask you to, but knowing that this, and much worse, has been the normal experience of women and children down the generations.

Many people, men and women, shy away from the word, the concept, of 'power'. And no wonder we reject the idea of power over others. The power that wishes to dominate and control. The power that uses fear, raised voices, anger and violence. The power that needs to make others small and weak and powerless in order to believe in its own power. The power that tramples over people to get to the top and keeps them 'below', keeps them down.

I now feel that I can choose a different form of power. I used to think that quiet people have no power. I have been learning that the opposite is true. There is a deep power in listening and observing.

As I grew up, I discovered other ways, ones I am also now leaving behind. Through natural aging, which I choose not to fight, the power of being a physically attractive young woman is no longer available to me. I also now know that the internal beauty of a person does not age; in fact, it often shines all the more brightly as time goes on.

The power I wish to step into, the path I have chosen to follow, is of power within. Power within is different. It chooses to start inside. To examine the heart. To connect with the good within each of us. We are all different. Yet, we each desire the same basic necessities: food, shelter, warmth, love. We each have the capacity to give and receive love if it is not frightened or frozen out of us. And even then, there is the seed, the capacity there to love. It may need the most tender and hands-off nurturing to dare to even think about breaking out from the tight bud — to dare to blossom may be a step too far at the beginning.

When the power within does emerge, and is used in the collaborative, feminine way, it supports others: together we rise. Male or female, or however we may see ourselves, this approach brings a balance of yin and yang, feminine and masculine, reflection and action, allowing the best of each to shine forth together.

The power that I invite you step into, gently and with ease and grace, is a quiet power. A power that can move mountains and change the world, one small step at a time. A practical power that helps us be true to ourselves and to operate from that place — at work, in our businesses, in relationships of all sorts.

I want to share with you a little of my journey from frightened child to where I am today, a woman who is happy and proud to stand in her power as an elder, as someone who has lived a full life (with plenty still to come, however long or short my years turn out to be), and who has wisdom to offer those who choose to hear these words.

Reflecting on my journey of rediscovering my inner power, and of choosing to step into that power, I see a pattern, an ebb and flow: Incoming waves that have carried me, enabled me to be more, to dare more, to stand up and speak. Then the waves recede, leaving me feeling a little lost, maybe even powerless for a while. After each wave, I look around and see that I am a little higher up that metaphorical beach than before, even if I feel stranded, abandoned by the power that carried me so effortlessly.

After this pattern repeats, over and over, I learn to relax, to await the next wave. However long it takes, one always appears. Like a surfer on the ocean, I begin to learn to read the currents and the sea.

I notice the signs of the next wave coming in from afar — to notice as it builds, to choose the best place, the one where I can most easily take off and use the power of the ocean to move me forward again.

Deep and Slow

In the summer of 2019, after I had booked my trip to travel to New Zealand to visit my family there for the first time since 2006, and to speak at the HerStory conference in Wellington, I had a profound experience.

Often, when I most need a soulful connection. I forget. I forget to ask, I forget to tune in, I forget to listen to the messages I receive. This time I did remember, and asking delivered a powerful message for me.

One night in August, I woke suddenly in the night with an excruciating headache, unlike any previous experience. I got up, checking as I went for the signs of a stroke: my face was fine, as was my speech (as far as I could tell), I could easily lift both arms above my head.

I did have a strange dizziness, a light-headed feeling, and a sensation of numbness around my lips. I took one painkiller and went back to bed. In the UK we are fortunate to have our wonderful National Health Service (NHS), but that means it is hard to get an appointment to see a doctor. I tried but nothing was available.

So, I just rested. That severe headache had gone but the other feelings were the same the next day and I managed to get an emergency appointment. I was referred straight away for tests at the nearest hospital. My husband drove me there, we were told that I would be there until the evening, so he went home and then made the return journey, a round trip of fifty miles each time, to pick me up again later.

There I had various scans and tests, all of which were negative. I was advised that the only way to be totally sure that I had not had a bleed in the brain was to undergo a lumbar puncture. As I was lying on my side the hospital bed, as the doctor sitting behind me prepared to insert the needle to draw out some spinal fluid, I remembered to ask. I decided to call on Source for help, and specifically my connection with the ocean.

I immediately received a wonderful sense of being supported. I heard the song of humpback whales and saw images of them floating in the water between the ocean depths and the surface. So graceful and such huge creatures.

I had my eyes shut and the sun light was streaming through the window so the colour through my eyelids was red/orange. I saw a huge whale's eye looking at me with such love and tenderness.

The very same day, a kayaker took some stunning photos and video of humpback whales feeding off the coast of Cornwall, a rare occurrence here. A coincidence, or part of the message?

The procedures found nothing of concern to the doctors. As I was told, it is rather unfortunate that the main side effect of a lumbar puncture is severe headaches.

I needed to take a long time to rest and recuperate, most of the rest of August in fact. I took the opportunity to connect in meditation, with my inner wisdom, and with the power of the mother whale. She gave me this message: 'Deep and Slow'.

This feels the perfect recipe for rest and recuperation. And it has stayed with me as a mantra for going through my daily life.

Later when I was able to walk out the cliffs again, I asked the fulmars (one of my favourite birds, related to the albatross) who soar and sweep around the cliff ledges for their insight: 'Use the uplift, go with the flow' was their message.

My mantra expanded: 'Deep and slow. Use the uplift. Go with the flow.' As I complete this book now, in early spring 2020, the

fulmars have just this week offered me
another phrase: 'Be bold'. One I am still
sitting with just now.

Being bold has often felt too much for me
during my life, and yet, as I write that, and
think about the memories I will be sharing
with you now, I can see that I have been
bold, many times over.

Childhood memories

Here are some snippets of memories, and some stories of parts of my journey through this life so far, of sometimes riding the wave, and at others feeling stranded, or becalmed. These are the memories I hold; adults who were around me at the time the events occurred may well recall them quite differently, even see my recollections as incorrect, so I offer them here as stories. Stories with messages, even if the details are inaccurate or even fictional.

My very earliest memory is of the day my baby brother came home from hospital. I was nearly two and a half years old. I remember my mother giving me my brother to hold as I sat in the back of the car. I felt so proud to be entrusted to hold him. My mother was probably very wise, knowing that involving me would help me feel she was not abandoning me when she needed to care for the new baby.

Truly a moment when this tiny girl, at two and a half still really a baby herself, felt responsible for another, and felt a power of the most tender and loving kind.

I have very few photos of my childhood, or of any period of my life until quite recent years. I am including a few here for you even though they may not be the precise age that I am writing about.

Around four years old – I already loved cats

Another memory: I am very young, five or six, I don't remember exactly. (My sister remembers me being about three years old, so this is one of my inaccurate memories). I have been very ill, for what seems like a long time, with rheumatic fever. I am so weak that my mother has to carry me downstairs in the mornings where I lie on a daybed.

My little brother can run around and play outside, and I am very envious. A doctor comes regularly to look at me and gives me injections with an enormous needle. One day our old cat climbs in through the window above my bed and lands in the bowl of pudding I am eating. Very messy.

One night, I am alone and scared. I call out for my mother, but she doesn't come. Maybe she can't hear me. I doze on and off, but I am sure I am awake when I hear a voice. It speaks to me, clearly, with a message, one that is comforting and that is to influence me greatly later in my life.

If only I hadn't forgotten that message for so many years. Or, maybe that was the way it was meant to be, in the same way that as babies we come into the world forgetting where we are from and how we come to be here.

I don't know when I forgot hearing the message and the words the voice spoke to me. It was a very long time before I recalled even hearing the voice. When I did, I was frustrated for quite a few more years by not remembering the words.

Eventually, after some difficult times, which proved to also contain gifts that transformed my life, I did remember one day, in a meditation.

The words were: "You are safe, my child."

At first, I heard the voice as a deep one, and wondered whose it was, assuming that it was someone outside myself: God, Jesus, an angel? Later, I came to the realisation that the voice was from my higher self, the source of my inner wisdom, and of my power. The self that is connected to the collective consciousness of all that is.

Even though I may not have realised the significance as a small child, I think I knew how important this experience was, and how much power it held for me. However, for many years this knowing, and that voice, was lost to me.

I remember being very frustrated when I was ill, as I was not allowed to start school. This may have been due to another illness, when my brother and I both caught measles at the same time. Either way, I so, so wanted to go. We moved house, to Cornwall, and I went to school at last. My little brother was very envious and wanted to come, too.

My sister told me just recently, that my mother sent me to school on that first day in a 'very smart' matching coat and hat. She probably bought it in a charity shop as we had very little money in those days.

I have no memory of this at all – rather strangely. Sue says I came home with the hat in my hand, and threw it on the floor, saying "I am never wearing that again!"

We can only think that I was teased at school for wearing a hat, who knows? The photo below may or may not have been the same coat, although I think I am a little younger here.

A smart winter coat

Looking at these black and white photos now, I wonder what that younger version of me was thinking.

Here is another memory that has stayed with me. I think it was the same school, my first.

I am at school. I don't know anyone. The other children are not very friendly, and all seem to know each other. The teachers are scary. One day the class (it may have been the whole school, as it was just a tiny village school) are brought together. Someone has been smearing excrement on the white walls of the cubicles in the outside toilets. No one owns up. I am called in by myself to see the headmistress. She says: "It was you — someone saw you." "No, no, it wasn't me!" I keep saying. "Yes, it was," she says. "You will be punished."

We are all called together again. A teacher takes me by the hand and leads me to the front. The headmistress has a ruler in her hand. "Hold out your hand." She takes my hand and hits it several times with the ruler.

I have no memories of what happened next or if my parents were told. I simply remember the injustice of being punished for something I didn't do. This was a low point, a time of losing touch with that power I knew instinctively as a baby and toddler. A time of feeling misjudged, ignored, ill-treated.

All together I attended five primary schools between the ages of six and 11. I have many memories of happy experiences. And many of always being the new girl, the outsider, the one who didn't fit in. And of always leaving friends behind and having to start again. Once I learned to read, books were my friends, companions and refuge.

Another thing that made me 'different' was that my father was ill. He had suffered some injuries during the war, leading to emphysema, chronic bronchitis and possibly a collapsed lung. I was taught to say, when asked: "What does your father do?", to say he was an invalid.

The photo below is a 'school photo' taken when I was attending Padstow County Primary School. In those days it was in the old Victorian stone building, now converted to apartments.

Aged about seven

The photo on the back cover must have been taken the following year. I think my mother had just cut my hair, before that I wore it long, most of the time in plaits, as in the picture above. I remember her simply cutting them off one day, and then tidying the ends up a little afterwards.

In 1964 I was looking forward to beginning secondary school. We had moved again, to Tywardreath in Cornwall (via several other places in the intervening years). Fowey Grammar School was a wonderful building overlooking the river, built of brick, unusual for that area of Cornwall. There were beautiful views from some of the classrooms. It was very tempting to look out the window at the river, with the boats going about their business, and daydream. (The school has sadly been demolished and replaced by apartments.)

The headmaster knew every one of the 150 pupils by name. There was an old-fashioned library with shelves of books up to the ceiling. I loved that library so much; it became a special place for me. Such power in the words, in the worlds created within those books.

I knew a few fellow pupils, as I had spent one term at the primary school in Tywardreath, although I still felt new to the area.

It was that early teenage time of intense friendships and equally intense fallings-out; of cliques and groups, whispers and giggles. I remember lining up in physical education class. At first, I was one of the smaller ones. I soon had a growth spurt, and an equivalent early maturity, and moved up the line.

Bullying began, and I retreated to my companions: books. I remember the headmaster coming into the library one lunchtime. "Hello, what are you doing here?" "Just reading sir." "What is the book?" " 'The Lord of the Rings.' " "A big book at your age." (I was 12.) I felt seen by him speaking to me, powerful even. I would not have used that word then, but reflecting now, I remember often feeling that I was invisible. And that, when I was out of someone's sight, they would forget I even existed.

So, when my headmaster knew my name, and took time to talk to me, that did feel an affirmation that I mattered in some way, and therefore I possessed a sort of power.

I imagine he probably guessed I wasn't happy, but he moved on soon, to the bigger grammar school in St Austell. Later, when my mother found out about the bullying (through asking me why there was blood on my white school blouse, which was from the pins the girls would prick me with from behind while we were sitting in our rows in class), then I moved to that school, too.

On a school trip to France, I remember a conversation with a lovely young English teacher about bullying. "You do know that they are jealous of you?" "Who, me?"

"Yes, you are elegant and beautiful, and the boys all love you." I think of my beloved older sister, whom I look up to and feel is truly elegant and beautiful, and I feel like the ugly duckling before she realises she is becoming a swan.

My first passport photo

My sister tells me how she remembers me then, that I was a quiet, shy girl who never did anything very much, however much she tried to encourage me when she was around. (My sister is eight years older and left home at 15 to attend college, so I didn't see very much of her as I was growing up).

This was also the time for me of the beginnings of a realisation that in this culture, a young, attractive girl had a sort of power. This seemed frightening to me. I did not understand the sexual feelings I seemed to evoke.

Such complicated 'territory' to navigate as a teenager, with the changes brought about by hormones. The arrival of puberty and menstruation, which my mother referred to as 'the curse'. All those turbulent emotions and wanting to be 'in love' whatever that meant.

I feel fortunate to have been growing up in those days in many ways and not to be dealing with all that modern technology and social media brings to young people today. And yet, those things also bring gifts, and as always, we each have our own path to tread.

Some thoughts on introversion

Many people speak of how they resist the very idea that they have power. I have no way of truly remembering the thoughts of my young self as a teenager. It was very much later that I began to learn about introverts and extroverts and the different qualities each brings to the world, and that each of us can experience different shades of these qualities, different combinations, at different times.

Realising that my 'default' is introversion has been extraordinarily helpful. For me the simple distinction is that introverts like to recharge their energy by retreating, spending time alone: with books, in nature, meditating, writing, painting. These activities enable me to go out again — to interact enthusiastically with people in the world, to teach groups, to speak at conferences and meetings.

Extroverts tend to recharge by going out, by socializing. Being in a big group of

people all talking, laughing, having fun —
this is where they gain their energy.

For me, there is a connection here with
the different sort of power I wrote about
earlier: "... a quiet power. A power that
can move mountains and change the
world, one small step at a time. A practical
power that helps us be true to ourselves
and to operate from that place — at work,
in our businesses, in relationships of all
sorts."

Exploring this further with people in my
community, my support team, the concept
of 'source power' began to emerge. When
I meditated and sat with this, I was
reminded of the natural wells in the city
of Wells, in Somerset.

Until I visited them, I had not imagined
what they are: deep pools within which
the water bubbles up from deep down in
the earth. That image has brought me joy
ever since, a sense of the effortless
bubbling up of a joyful power.

Growing up and university

When did I begin to realise that I had power? Even as one of the 'quiet ones'? When did I begin to dare to blossom?

Reflecting, I can see that this happened in stages as I navigated my way through life as best I could. Some of the milestones are common to most people. My first serious relationship, my first love, was in a way empowering. Yet, the ideal of 'romantic love' encourages us to give away our power willingly to another, believing that we are incomplete without our 'other half'.

I now know it is unfair to place that burden of expectation on one person, and that I can be whole entirely by myself. In fact, for a truly adult version of love to flourish, each partner needs to be in that place of independence, of self-sufficiency, so they can allow themselves to be vulnerable and to love another enough to share their life with them.

Other things, fortunately, are specific to me, such as being in a bad road accident when I was studying for my A-levels (the final school exams in England, before moving on to employment, college or university). This resulted in me spending several weeks in hospital, and the whole of the summer vacation at home convalescing.

I have a memory of exerting my power when a doctor offered me tranquilisers to cope with exam stress and I tore up the prescription, determined that I would not rely on pills. I know now that these can be very helpful in many circumstances, yet even my young self then was sure they weren't for me at that time. Another wave, bringing me a little higher, a little closer to truly reconnecting with my inner power.

I left home to go to university, with all the excitement of new friendships and relationships, the joy, and the pressure, of studying and exams. I chose the University of Reading, not far outside London, partly because there was a direct train route from my home in Cornwall. It also had a well-respected geography department, including a charismatic professor, Peter Hall who was well known in the field of town planning at the time. Looking up his name now, I discovered he continued to have an illustrious career as an 'urbanist' and was knighted in 1998, dying in 2014.

I was extremely fortunate to have been the right age to go to university in the era of grants that did not need to be repaid. I was quite frugal with my money, and I remember my mother giving me £20 most terms, which went quite a long way in those days (the early 1970s).

In my first year I lived in a student room in a traditional hall of residence. In those days they had shared bathrooms, the rooms simply had a bed, a desk and a chair. Meals were provided in a huge dining room. As often happens, I met people who became lasting friends during our university days and later.

The second two years were in a newer block of student 'flats', a group of rooms with, again shared bathrooms, and a fully equipped kitchen where we cooked our own meals. In those days all the halls were single sex, although often you would meet boyfriends in the corridor.

When I first went away to university, I had a 'school-days sweetheart', who went to Liverpool University. It was a long journey from Reading, but I visited a few times. By the end of our first year we had begun to grow apart, maybe a natural part of growing up. Sad in some ways. In others simply one of those forks in the road. Who knows where we would both be if we had chosen differently?

My degree is in geography, combining my curiosity about the world around me and my love of people. In the second year, we had to specialise in either physical or human geography. I chose the latter and loved learning about archaeology, history, and why settlements grew up where they did. There was a little economics and sociology as well, all of which I found fascinating. I can't say I enjoyed writing essays too much, nor exams, yet, looking back I can see how much I grew up and changed during those three years.

There are very few photos of that time, and they are too poor quality to reproduce here. One that brings back poignant memories was taken just after our final exams in June 1974, at a gathering in a student house before we all went to a dance. I am wearing one of those flower pattern long dresses that were so popular then (in fact all the women in the photo are), and have long shiny brown hair, with no fringe at that time. In the photograph I have my plate of salad balanced on my lap – as I remember there were rather a lot of us squeezed into the room to eat together. I look quite wistful, again I wonder what that young woman, that younger me, was thinking.

I think I was already aware of what a magical and privileged time we had all shared together over the previous three years; of how much I had learned; of how much I had changed. And of how different life would be as we all dispersed in different directions.

Travels and adventures

When that sheltered existence as a student ended, I found myself unable to get the sort of job I had hoped for using my degree.

I returned to live at home, feeling very low. I decided to set out on a solo adventure to visit and work in New Zealand, where my sister and her young family had settled a few years earlier. I paid for it with the insurance money from the accident I had been involved in, which had finally come through after a lot of persistence.

In those days the most cost-effective way to travel was by sea, if you had plenty of time to spare, the one thing I was rich in as an unemployed graduate. The cheapest fares were in a six-berth cabin below the water line of the ship, with no porthole for a glimpse of daylight.

At that age (21) it was all an adventure. There were many young people from Australia and New Zealand on board, returning from their travels in Europe. Even though there were various classes of passengers, some in the upper deck suites, travelling for pleasure rather than to get from A to B, as we were, we all had access to the same places to eat, and the same entertainment.

As we set off across the stormy Bay of Biscay travelling south (it was September when I left the UK), I loved the experience of being at sea on a long voyage. I avoided seasickness by staying out on deck in the fresh air as much as possible, and drinking the recommended 'cure' of a measure each of port and brandy in one glass. (Recommended by the bar staff, anyway. I am not sure how effective that was in reality.)

I soon made friends amongst the other young passengers, and we sometimes socialized with the crew as well, who were mostly from Greece, where the ship was registered, and some from the Philippines.

At that time the Suez Canal was closed due to conflict in the area, so the ship headed south down the coast of Africa, calling in at the Canaries, and then Cape Town. Short runs ashore for a few hours were arranged, and then we were back underway across the Indian Ocean to Perth, then Melbourne, Sydney and Auckland.

It is a wonderful way to travel: arriving in a new port, watching as we docked before disembarking (or sometimes being taken ashore in small boats), seeing the sights and sounds of a strange land. Then boarding again and waving farewell as we sailed.

All the ports were fascinating, and I loved Sydney. The harbour is of course one of the great sights of the world: the Sydney Opera House (which had only opened a year earlier); the bridge; the beauty of the harbour, with all the inlets and promontories. (Little did I know that two years later I would be back there, working in a hotel on Cremorne Point).

I also loved the long stretches at sea, being out on deck in all conditions, with the weather gradually warming up as we journeyed south. We watched out for dolphins, and as we neared the equator, flying fish — amazing creatures, skimming over the waves to escape the predators below.

We went through the obligatory 'crossing the line' ceremony for those travelling over that invisible line, the Equator, for the first time. There was always plenty to do, but also opportunities to escape to a quiet corner of the deck and read, or simply watch the ocean go by.

Once we arrived in Auckland, I discovered that some sort of industrial action was going on, so the ship did not continue to Lyttleton in the South Island, close to where my sister lived (and still does) in Christchurch. So, I had to change my plans and travel by train to Wellington and then by ferry to Picton. My brother-in-law very kindly made the long drive from Christchurch to meet me there.

I loved spending time with him and my sister and their three daughters. The younger two are twins, and spending time with the three girls, who I think were still all under five, taught me the realities of family life. My sister later teased them, saying the reason that I have no children is due to their bad behaviour when I visited. That isn't true, but one of them told me she believed it for years.

I spent around nine months in New Zealand, working in hotel jobs that supplied live-in accommodation, at opposite ends of the country. First in Te Anau, in the mountains of the far south, and then in the Bay of Islands, in the subtropical north. I loved both places, and the journeys through the spectacular scenery of New Zealand on what were then rather rickety buses. Travelling alone, I learned to chat with people along the way and enjoyed many interesting conversations.

In the hotel where I worked in Te Anau, all the staff were local or Australian except me. There is a friendly teasing relationship between people from the Australia and New Zealand, and every so often they would add in a 'Pommie' joke so I wouldn't feel left out.

Christchurch, NZ 1975 – a reflective moment

At the hotel in the Bay of Islands there were many more Maori workers. I remember chatting to the kitchen staff, especially a large motherly woman who made me very tasty cheese and tomato sandwiches one day when I was going out somewhere. We also would join in singing around a fire on the beach, eating big slices of watermelon.

I had many new experiences and made numerous friends, some of whom are still in touch to this day. One of them, Gabrielle, gave me a lift back to Auckland when we both left the hotel, driving along the gravel roads, we had no radio, so we sang songs instead. Mostly from Leonard Cohen for reasons I cannot remember, belting out 'So long Marianne….' at the tops of our voices.

The return voyage, on the same ship, was equally interesting — across the Pacific to Fiji, Acapulco, through the Panama Canal, to Fort Lauderdale in Florida, and then back across the Atlantic.

This experience, what I suppose would now be called a gap year, was nothing unusual — and that is exactly the reason for sharing it. I was stepping into my power: my power as a young, attractive woman.

I think I was unaware of how much of the power I felt I possessed was to do with being young and female, and unaware of how that was dependent on those more powerful than I, mostly men, 'allowing' me some degree of power.

In some ways that ignorance may have helped me navigate the world. In other ways, it may have led me into situations that I know now I was lucky to come through without any serious consequences.

Making my own mistakes and learning from them were part of the process, the rites of passage, of growing up.

Like virtually every woman I know, I have tales of harassment and sexual assault. I am choosing not to share details of those here. When I was young, they were almost accepted, and certainly expected. A statement that sounds so sad to me now. My personal view is that much has changed, improved, for some women. In so many parts of the world this is not true, yet at least awareness is growing.

On the other hand, even in privileged 'western' societies, young women are growing up in what appears to be a regressive culture where they must contend with pornography and all the other pressures. There has been much written over recent years and by so many people more qualified than I to discuss and comment.

For me, there are so many big issues where I can feel powerless. The only way forward for me is to begin where I am, right here. To stand in my power within, and to be the best 'me' I can, in the knowledge that from there ripples can, will, spread out to others.

Losing my way

I returned to the UK in June 1975 feeling full of joy, with a lovely suntan, and not knowing what to do next. I found myself back at home with my parents and began applying for 'proper' jobs again. I found summer work in two different local pubs. I had fun, worked hard and enjoyed socialising.

And I felt I had lost my way. In desperation, as autumn approached, I did what I thought I would never do: applied for a place on a post-graduate teacher training course, a one-year programme, in Southampton.

There I was deeply lonely and unhappy. I see now how I could have chosen not to be, but at that time I felt at the mercy of circumstances. I missed university life, but the college was nothing like that, even though I made some good friends.

I had trouble finding somewhere to live as I applied too late to get a place in the halls of residence. I arranged to rent a room in a private house, but when I arrived the owner had decided she wanted two of us to share the room — which didn't work for either of us. For some reason that I cannot recall, I was the one to move out. I found a bedsit in another private house, one with very strict rules: one bath a week, visitors not allowed after a certain time in the evening.

I found the course — learning to teach primary school children — a challenge, and interesting. However, there seemed to be very few teaching posts to apply for, at home in Cornwall or elsewhere, and a gradual realisation dawned that I had made a mistake. I began to comfort-eat, and drink, and at my lowest point put on a lot of weight (for me, anyway).

One day I found myself sitting in my room crying, with a large bottle of cider and a bumper bag of peanuts for company. My goodness, I had certainly turned my back on my true power then, given it away entirely.

When I returned home at the end of that first term, I thought very carefully, and decided to leave the course. It was a foolish choice, in many ways, two more terms and I would have had another qualification to my name, with a potential, at least, for employment. I don't remember how much it influenced my decision, but my mother was planning a visit to New Zealand, and, although I am sure my mother wouldn't have put any pressure on me, I knew I could be useful at home while she was away. Anyway, I wrote to the college and received a very understanding reply, saying that it was important to do what was right for me.

Another low point, and yet, with a hint of a new uplift, a fresh wave coming soon. Taking a decision about what I didn't want allowed me to move towards something else, even if I did not yet know what that would be.

During that winter I enrolled at a local college to gain some secretarial skills, in case they could be useful. Those days of typewriters seem so far away now. When I was at university, we were taken to visit the mainframe computer, which was housed in a huge building under specially controlled conditions. The closest we had to a computer was an adding machine we used in statistics classes.

I reconnected with some old school friends and began to build a new a social life. One of the places we would go was a country club near Padstow, where the disco was sometimes run by Rick Stein, who had just set up what was to become the famous Seafood Restaurant. (Later he became well known in the UK as a TV chef).

When he advertised jobs for waitresses for the summer of 1976, I applied and was offered a post six evenings a week. The staff accommodation was an old-style caravan near St Merryn. I didn't drive, so when my friend who had started there with me very soon decided to leave, Rick gave me lifts to work.

During that summer I met my future husband, who was working as a lifeguard, and as an auxiliary coastguard. Not long after we met, he saved the life of an elderly man who had been swept off the rocks around the corner from Harlyn Bay. In those days there was only one lifeguard, and I had to call the coastguard for help on the radio. That man, Wilf Kingdon, was one of the few who came back and thanked Dave after he recovered. He kept in touch for several years, and later gave Dave a copy of a book he knew would be appreciated (about shipwrecks around the Cornish coast).

Wilf included two photos in the front of the book, one of Dave with the 'torpedo' equipment that he took with him when he swam out to the rescue. The other is of himself on the same rocks where he was swept off – and underneath he wrote:

"Dave Lunnen risked his life to save mine of Sunday, July 11th, 1976"

For anyone who remembers 1976 in the UK, it was a famously hot, dry summer: glorious weather to be on the beach all day and working in the evenings. Dave had an old Spitfire sports car, and we rarely had to put the roof up.

The Seafood Restaurant was on the top floor of a big building, and most of the time I worked on the middle floor, where we served good-quality American-style steak burgers. Several nights a week there was live music from local players, and it became a popular place with my social circle. It was a magical summer.

I was still applying for jobs and went for a few interviews. And I had also booked another trip to New Zealand, to leave in late September, again by sea.

*The summer of 1976, at The Seafood
Restaurant in Padstow*

By the time the summer ended, Dave and I
had fallen in love. I set off on my travels,
not knowing whether this was a sweet
summer romance or something more
serious. I had an inkling straight away,
though — before I left, in fact. My mother
drove me to Southampton, and I was
ready to board the ship the next day.

When I phoned Dave to chat before I left,
he said he wanted to see me one more
time before our long separation. So, he
drove up from Cornwall and met us at
what was already and has been ever since

a favourite pub, the Green Dragon. This is not far from my birthplace of Lyndhurst in the ancient New Forest national park.

In the Triumph Spitfire, just before sailing

We had lunch, and my mother set off home. We somehow tied my luggage onto the Spitfire, and off we went to Southampton.

We have another photo of me (too fuzzy to share here) sitting on one of the large, mushroom-shaped bollards on the docks with the ship in the background, just before we had to say goodbye.

On reflection, that time was an interesting point in the ebb and flow of my inner power. I hadn't cancelled my trip (the thought had never crossed my mind), even though I knew I would miss Dave.

Our separation brought many gifts. With no email then, we wrote by airmail, two or three letters a week, with very occasional (and expensive) phone calls. We still treasure the letters today.

Dave and my mother became friends, and he visited her often, and was well looked after. In fact, I am pretty sure the two of them knew we would get married before I did. My power within felt in equilibrium. I didn't know what the future would hold, yet I had found a point to come home to. The Padstow area was where my family had lived for a year or so, and where I had attended primary school. Now I would be returning there after my travels.

The voyage, this time through the Mediterranean and the Suez Canal, enabling me to visit Cairo and the pyramids, was again full of discovery and new experiences. This time I had arranged to stop in Sydney for a while to spend more time in that beautiful city.

Until I arrived and disembarked with my luggage, I did not know that the Australian friend I had made on my previous visit to New Zealand had not received my letters with the date of my arrival due to a postal strike, and so had no idea I was due to arrive that day. I had to pull my heavy suitcase up the street from Central Quay until I found a telephone box to call her.

My friend's parents kindly let me stay with them while I looked for a hotel job. Despite warnings about the poor chances of employment at that time, and finding nothing advertised in the local papers, I began telephoning hotels, starting at the beginning of the alphabet. A few calls later, I was invited to an interview at the

Alexa Hotel at Cremorne Point, and a job offer followed.

I spent three months living and working with a view across Sydney Harbour to the Opera House and the bridge. Split shifts gave me time to explore in the afternoons, and I made longer trips on my days off. I went mostly by ferry, often via Central Quay to Manley, or by bus to the other beaches. I also visited restaurants, the cinema, the Opera House and the botanical gardens by myself, or with friends I made at work.

At Christmas I volunteered to work so others could spend time with family, turning down invitations to join them later, as I preferred quiet time to myself. I can feel the power of that choice again now. Choosing quiet time alone on Christmas Day goes against cultural norms, and it was such a beautiful decision for me that year.

Waitressing at The Alexa Hotel

Then I went on to New Zealand to spend some time with my family. In February that year, I decided to fly back to the UK early to be reunited with the man who had turned out to be the person with whom I would choose to spend the rest of my life.

Here we are on our wedding day, wearing wonderful 1970s styles. We just had very close family there, then held a big party for all our friends the following weekend, which was Easter.

Wedding day 2nd April 1977

Our honeymoon was a few days touring around Devon, with Dave's surfboard on the roof of the Spitfire. Appropriate in north Devon, at Woolacombe and Croyde, a little incongruous when we were driving around Dartmoor.

My mother also went away on a short trip, by some strange synchronicity, we met her in a layby in the Quantock Hills. She had stopped for a break and we happened to pass by in the opposite direction. We did a 'double-take' and turned around to say hello.

Starting Pydar Crafts and supporting my husband

Many more waves followed that lifted me, and ebbs that left me high and dry and floundering over the years after our marriage in April 1977. Wanting to stay in Cornwall and finding no jobs except seasonal ones, I started a small business making and selling copper enamel jewellery, later adding silk scarves and encaustic art, all exploring my love of colour that began as a small child and continues to this day.

My mother encouraged me, and indeed, she took up enamelling as well. She had trained in textile design and like many women, always found ways to use her skills to earn extra money for the family, to help us through some very difficult times.

As mentioned already, my father ended his war time service with health difficulties that meant that — after a long struggle and lots of persistence by my mother he began to receive a war pension, which made things easier for them.

This upbringing meant I had been brought up to be resourceful: my mother had designed knitting patterns and knitted up examples for magazines. Later she bought and sold antique prints and maps. She also hand-coloured these, and my first 'pocket money job' was colouring the borders of the maps. I gradually became more proficient and graduated to completing the whole map, then the prints as well.

So, I built up my own business, which I named 'Pydar Crafts' from the name of the area where we lived. On the maps I used to colour for pocket-money it was called, in the naming convention for the old administrative divisions: 'Pydar Hundred'.

Over a period of fifteen years I developed Pydar Crafts into a profitable business - working hard, working harder, then working too hard. Not being aware of valuing myself, of self-care, I pushed myself to a breaking point. In some ways it was a time of stepping into my power, up to a point. It was also a time of surrendering, or not seeing, choices that I could make.

A lot of it was great fun, and, looking back I realise how much I learned – by trial and error – about not only creating the crafts to sell, but also the marketing and sales aspects of running a small business. Not to mention other necessary skills such as keeping records and completing tax returns.

I met some wonderful people and sold my work all over the world, even in the days before online selling became so easy.

I could only ever afford an old car, and for several years I had a Renault 4, a very idiosyncratic car, with a back seat that folded flat and plenty of room for all my boxes of stock and tables.

It had a problem with the fuel system and would grind to a halt every so often. I became proficient at jumping out with my screwdriver, dismantling the carburettor, cleaning it out, and reassembling it.

Other drivers, mostly men, would often stop and offer to help, and would be quite taken aback when I assured them that I was able to deal with the problem myself. I admire that feisty young woman I was then; I am not sure I would be so confident now.

My husband Dave has also always run his own businesses, usually connected in some way with the sea. He loves surfing, diving, fishing.

In fact, to tell the story of his long and varied career would take another book, maybe he will write that one day.

He is almost ten years older than me and was divorced when we met. At that time, and for many years after we married, it was a great sadness to him that he was estranged from his two daughters.

Not very many years ago, his eldest daughter made contact, and we now see her and Dave's two granddaughters several times a year. Having decided not to have children, I suddenly found myself with a new extended 'step-family', a great joy.

Dave and I are very different characters, many would say total opposites. I know I have learned a lot from Dave over the years.

In staying together all this time we have needed to continually adapt and accommodate each other's needs, and to agree when to disagree. And to cope when that agreement sometimes seemed impossible to find.

Somehow, despite, or maybe because of, our differences, and our different interests, here we are, soon to celebrate our 43rd wedding anniversary.

During this time of setting up my crafts business, my father had a stroke. We had no telephone in those days, and I remember my mother driving over from the south coast of Cornwall to tell me.

Later he tried to take his own life by swallowing painkillers. I am sorry, ashamed, to say that I have very little memory of that time.

Quite recently my sister sent me a copy of a letter our father had written to her in New Zealand. In it he told her that he had wanted to spare our mother the 'burden' of caring for him as she had done for her own mother.

Not long after that they moved from the big family house where we had all lived since I was ten or eleven, to a smaller single storey bungalow, quite near where I live now.

I think things were better there for a while, and my mother developed a social life. She belonged to the Embroiderers Guild and passed on her skills to other women in the groups she attended.

She and my aunt went on holidays together sometimes, while my father stayed in a nursing home for respite care.

My aunt didn't drive but loved walking – she explored a large portion of the coastal footpath around England over the years. My mother couldn't walk so far as she had a heart problem. They made a good team with my aunt being dropped off at the beginning of a walk and my mother meeting her at the other end, having visited a church or a scenic spot along the way.

One day in the summer of 1985, my mother phoned early one morning, to tell me she had found my father dead from an overdose. Despite telling my sister he wouldn't do it again, and without leaving a note, he had succeeded this time.

It is sad when someone feels that is the only choice open to them, but it was his choice. In some ways he did use his own power to make that decision.

They had been married and stayed together through all the difficult times, for over forty years. Getting through war time, post-war rationing, bringing up a family, all while coping with my father's health problems. He may well have experienced post traumatic stress as well as the physical effects of his injuries.

As well as the sad memories, I have many happy ones and choose to focus on those.

My mother enjoyed her creative life, and her trips around the country, by herself and with my aunt. She also went to Europe a few times with my brother before he married. And to New Zealand to visit my sister and her family.

My mother, me and my sister at our brother's wedding in 1990

Changing times and a wakeup call

The economic recession of 1991 hit my business, many of my wholesale customers ceased ordering and my income dropped.

At the same time, I needed a change, and I was prompted to look at possibilities. I wanted to return to academic study, and I would have loved to have become a student at Plymouth University, but it was too big a commitment in travel time and cost.

So, in the end I chose remote study with the Open University and a master's in education. The first module was on gender and education, a mini-women's studies course that opened my eyes and reminded me again of my power and how and where I might be giving it away.

I loved the sheer joy of learning for learning's sake, and of attending a summer school (the regular tutorials were in Bristol, too far to travel every month). Summer school: a whole week of being a 'real' student in residence at Nottingham University. Meeting new people from different backgrounds, making new friends who stayed in touch for years. Magic.

To pay for the fees I started a job in Bodmin, with a newly established research branch of a London-based consultancy. This was my first experience of office work, an eye-opener after 15 years of self-employment.

In some ways, I was surrendering power to an employer. Yet the security of a regular, if small, salary was also gaining power for myself. Rapid growth of the staff team and new responsibilities as a manager brought learning, and stress.

From being self-employed and flexible, even if very busy and pushing myself hard, I now found myself in full-time employment, and studying on a post-graduate course with deadlines and exams.

How ironic that when I visited my doctor to ask for advice on dealing with stress at work that she should say: "I was glad to see you were coming in today, as I have to tell you the result of your smear test [Pap test] shows abnormalities, and you need a follow-up at the hospital."

I think I joked along the lines of, "Thanks a lot, that has helped my stress level no end." And in fact, I wasn't particularly worried. I knew that many women had abnormal results, which prove not to be anything serious.

I don't know why it took so long, but my referral for a colposcopy investigation took from March to May to come through. My mother drove me to the hospital, as the instructions were not to drive home afterwards.

A couple of days later, while I was at home after leaving work because of severe pain after the procedure, there was a call from the surgery, asking me to come in straight away.

As I drove myself the few miles to Padstow, the radio news came on with the announcement that John Smith, then leader of the Labour Party, had died suddenly. Somehow that added to the surreal nature of the experience.

I sat in shock as my doctor told me I had cervical cancer and required a radical hysterectomy and possibly radiotherapy. One of my first questions was, "Can I speak to someone else who has been through this?"

My doctor's reply was that she could not give me any names due to patient confidentiality. A few days later, I did find a phone helpline where I could talk to a nurse and ask many of the questions that were troubling me.

I searched all the information available, but very little was published specifically about cervical cancer, and it was hard to meet and talk to people with experience of a similar diagnosis. (This was before online networking had become so easy and such a powerful way of connecting.)

On the day of my diagnosis, I bought a journal to write my feelings and thoughts in, somehow knowing I just had to record the experience.

This journal became my friend and confidant. There I could express my true feelings, and my fears. The things I didn't want to share with my family. As I now know, many cancer patients find they are protecting their families, not wanting to "burden" them with the true extent of their worries.

My husband is wonderful at practical support, being a skilled engineer, and good at making all sorts of things. However, when I was diagnosed with cancer, I think he must have found it hard as he couldn't 'fix' what was wrong for me. I remember him saying that while I was in hospital, he found himself shedding a few tears, while stroking our cat who was sitting on his knee.

My treatment began with surgery, what is known as a radical or Wertheim's hysterectomy. This means that the womb is removed, also the ovaries, fallopian tubes, part of the cervix, and in my case some lymph nodes too as it appeared the cancer may have spread there.

I experienced severe pain after the surgery, my first real experience of this. I know now how subjective pain is, and that doctors sometimes do not seem to understand this.

During my first night after surgery, I was sure my mother was sitting by my bed, there in the hospital, singing my favourite childhood lullaby, "I had a Little Nut Tree".

When she came to visit the next day, I told her this. She said she had been sending me love and healing thoughts. She hadn't thought about the lullaby for years, it was so beautiful that her thoughts arrived with me when I needed them most, and in the form of her singing.

My journal also proved very useful when I needed to go back to the doctors (my GP [general practitioner] and the hospital consultant) with questions about the chronic pain that persisted long after my surgery. And it became the starting point for the book I was later to write.

After my initial treatment I decided to find a way of helping others like me. I placed a request in the magazine published by the cancer support organisation that had helped me, and I began to receive letters with powerful stories from other women. I started compiling them into a book of women's stories. I had no idea how I would achieve what seemed like an impossible dream, getting the book into print.

I began approaching publishers, sending a synopsis and sample chapter. Some did reply with a polite rejection letter; others did not. I just knew this book had to be published. Self-publishing wasn't an easy option then — money had to be found to edit, design and print the books, which, when published, had to be stored somewhere. And then marketed.

Somehow, I no longer remember exactly how it came about, I was given the name and number of Melissa Hardie of Patton Press. She is also the founder of the Hypatia Trust, an educational charity that supports and promotes women's achievements.

After an initial telephone conversation, I visited Melissa's home in West Cornwall, full of books and cats, and wonderful things. We began working together. Melissa helped me obtain some sponsorship towards the publishing costs; I raised a small sum, too, and invested some money of my own.

Meanwhile, the stories were coming in: heart-rending, moving, inspiring, funny. I had many telephone conversations with each woman. Some I was able to visit in Cornwall, and I travelled to London to meet others. One person's husband came up with the title for the book: *Flying in the*

Face of Fear. Another woman offered a cover photo: of her wing-walking on a biplane piloted by her husband. As she said, after coming through cancer, nothing scared her any longer. They both contributed pieces for the book.

One woman I had spoken to several times died during the compilation of the book. Her husband wrote to me and gave his permission to share the words she had already written. He also offered to add a piece himself about the effects of her illness, and her death, on him. I was extremely grateful for this. I felt it was important to be able to share the whole range of experiences.

Yes, many people (even more now, over 25 years later) recover and not only survive but thrive afterwards, as I have done. Others do not survive, and this, too, can be a transformative process for them and their families, giving them precious time together that they may not have appreciated in the same way otherwise.

For the cover, in addition to the wonderful photo, I just knew it had to be purple. I am not sure why: I just knew it had to be that deep, rich colour. It was such a huge thrill when I collected my first box of books from Melissa and held a copy in my hands for the first time.

Book number one in 1998

Marketing a book was very different in those days — there were no online booksellers. Melissa helped me get the details out through her publishing contacts, and I visited local bookshops, learning a lot along the way. Some were prepared to buy copies from me as a local author, and others expected 'sale or return'.

I contacted local newspapers, sending out press releases to as many journalists as I could, and local radio stations.

Local press publicity photo by Mary Neale

I was interviewed on BBC Radio Cornwall by a young male reporter. He had obviously read at least some of the review copy I had sent him, as one of his questions was about his initial shock at the humour in the book. One of the women had called her chapter 'Tumour Humour.' As she explained, it signified the black humour that many of us find helps in difficult circumstances.

Many of the orders came straight to me, and I sent a personal letter with each book. Later, I often received replies with moving stories of how the book had helped women feel less alone after their diagnosis. I remember one of my first reactions on reading about someone's experience was relief: "Oh … it isn't just me that feels like that!" I gave away many copies to cancer charities, and others were bought by nurses to give to their patients.

Writing the book showed me the power of connections, the joy of community, the strength we have together. I have just recently (in 2019) sold the last copies of that book, though some are circulating secondhand, and I am so proud that I didn't give up in my seemingly impossible dream of publication.

Flying in the Face of Fear led to my first commissioned book: *The Essential Guide to Cervical Cancer* (published in 2010, with an updated edition in 2018) — an achievement I am proud of, as I am of an enthusiastic review by Susan Quilliam[i], a professional whose writing had helped me years earlier.

The experience of cancer, at first a huge blow, helped me access my own power in new ways. Part of this was learning to put my own needs first. I went back to work far too soon.

My employer was very generous and had kept me on full pay for several months during my treatment, but I didn't realise how ridiculous it was to be struggling to operate as normal in such severe pain.

One day I rang the office to say I would be in late, as I was in too much pain to drive. One of my colleagues answered and simply said, "Mary, you shouldn't be doing this. Stay at home."

So I did, for another six weeks, going on state sick pay, which, even though difficult financially, took the pressure off. During this time my employer realised how serious this was, and I was able to arrange to work from home several days a week, and to return to work gradually. (These days, that is usually arranged from the beginning after a serious illness).

I also began to reclaim my power from what had felt for a while like a medical conveyor belt. I felt as if I had been treated as a body part, not a person. I explored complementary therapies to help me cope with the chronic pain from my surgery, and the exhaustion — first acupuncture, and then reiki. Each practitioner I worked with helped me in their particular ways.

Moving on and another wakeup call

After a while I began to look for opportunities to use my research skills in a job helping people with health issues. I also began to volunteer for Macmillan Cancer Research, running workshops and giving talks.

I found a part-time post as research officer at Cornwall Community Health Council, at that time one of a network of statutory bodies that had the right to investigate patient concerns as a 'patients' watchdog'. The salary was lower there, so I continued to work part time in my other position with the research company.

Not long after I began this job, my mother experienced a severe stroke. I found her on the floor of her home, where she had lain for 24 hours, and then I followed the ambulance to the hospital. For some time, we did not know how severe her condition was, what she could understand, and whether she could communicate.

On the second day she gestured that she wanted to write something, so I found a pen and paper in my bag. The words she managed to write were: "Go home and rest." I cried and hugged her, knowing at least that my dearly beloved mother was still aware inside her now disabled body, and still as thoughtful and caring as ever.

I began a time of supporting her through hospital stays and then moving into a nursing home. More than one, in fact, as the first place closed with only one month's notice.

Even though I wasn't providing physical care, I was doing a lot: visiting, and taking my mother out in my car for outings. I was learning how to manage someone paralysed down her left side, to get her out of her wheelchair and into the car. Managing her finances, providing emotional support. Organising the sale of her home to pay the nursing home fees.

Along the way, we had some very special experiences together, conversations we would probably not have had in other circumstances, sharing things we could not have done had she died the day of her stroke. Even though she told me she would have preferred it that way, which I understood, I was so grateful for the gift she gave me by not leaving then.

My mother and I in conversation over dinner

I began learning to be a reiki healer myself, something that made a big difference to me personally, and it was also a joy to be able to offer healing to my mother when she asked, and to the matron of one of the nursing homes. I had learned to "get out of the way" and let the healing flow through me and was amazed when the matron's back greatly improved almost immediately.

Around this time my mother told me a story, one I have no memory of as I was still a baby when it happened, but one that has been very significant to me over the years.

One day, while our family were on holiday, my father took my sister to a local town, possibly to see some fireworks later that evening. I was too small to go, so my mother and I stayed at the caravan where we were staying. I think we were sitting outside, or maybe she was looking out of the window.

My mother saw a blue light, a ball of light I think was how she described it, that travelled along the valley in front of us. She said she watched it for some time, totally intrigued and perplexed as to what it could be. There was no noise.

It seemed to be 'interested' in the two of us. After a while it disappeared. When my father and sister returned, my mother asked if they had seen anything – they had not, and the firework display had not been visible from the caravan. So, we never did find out what it may have been.

When my mother told me the story, around the time I used reiki to help the matron of the nursing home, I told her that I often see a blue light when I am receiving or giving healing. In our conversation we decided that if I was ever to start a business offering this, I could call it 'Blue Light Healing'.

And we joked that this could have a double meaning: the matron's experience had been almost of immediate relief from her pain, as if she had been treated by an emergency service, with a blue light. And it could be that the blue light that visited us had a spiritual connection with this.

This was part of a new wave, a different sort of power within to explore, one connected with the greater universal consciousness.

I feel so privileged to have had the years with my mother, sadly she became more and more unwell and unhappy with her life in the nursing home. She had to move three times in six and a half years, each time an upheaval and with new people to get to know.

She had some trips to hospital as well. Once when being moved by a member of staff, she fell heavily, and another time, while I was there, she had an epileptic fit. This is not unusual for stroke patients, I know now. Frightening at the time, for both of us, and she thought she might be having another stroke.

Several times I offered her reiki and she seemed to enjoy it. One day my teacher, Liz, came in and we gave her a joint healing. I had my eyes closed most of the time, Liz told me later my mother didn't take her eyes off me, with a beautiful smile on her face.

Some of my other complementary therapy contacts also came in and offered their services: acupuncture and kinesiology both seemed to help in their different ways.

The last hospital visit was just after we had come back from an outing in my car together. We had been to a local reservoir, a pretty lake with tranquil water. We sat in the car and chatted as usual. I don't recall now if we had our coffee and biscuits.

My mother always travelled with her 'coffee bag' in the days when she drove around on holidays herself. Even for a morning out, she packed a flask of hot water, another containing milk. A little jar of coffee, another with sugar (brown of course). A tin with biscuits – her favourites were shortbread fingers and dark chocolate digestives.

So, when I was in charge of our trips out, I did the same. 'Mum's (or Grandma's) coffee bag' was famous in our family. The bag itself was one that my sister had brought back from a visit to a friend in Malta when she was just a teenager. The familiar ritual was a comforting return to 'normality' for my mother.

On this day, we enjoyed our conversation beside the lake. We returned to the nursing home, and we executed our now well-practised manoeuvres to get her out of the front seat of the car and into the wheelchair.

As we got inside and met the staff, my mother began to feel breathless. We went up to her room and she was put into bed, but it got worse, so an ambulance was called. One of the paramedics was someone I knew; it was good to see a familiar face – although I have huge respect for every paramedic for their skill and kindness.

The ambulance set off to the nearest hospital with an emergency department, with me again following in my car. It turned out she had suffered a pulmonary embolism – a blood clot in the lungs – another danger following a stroke. It was stabilised and she returned to the nursing home.

After that, my mother seemed to lose any remaining joy in life, and simply gave up. She had conversations with me, with the staff and with the doctors, asking to be 'put out of her misery'. To be given a pill so she could sleep. To be treated, as she would say, as well as 'you would treat an animal in pain.'

It was heart-breaking. At the same time, totally understandable. Eventually she stopped eating. She had decided that was the only control she had, the only power she had to make her choice.

It was hard. Hard to watch her fading away. Hard for the staff whose job it was to care for her. The staff loved her; she had become like an 'agony aunt' to them. Always ready to listen to their troubles. Full of suggestions: a balm that might soothe a baby's eczema; a herbal remedy that may cure a bad stomach.

When my mother did leave her tired body, on what she and I had begun to call her 're-birthday', she was more than ready to go. The previous day I had been to see her. She whispered to me (her voice had begun to go as a result of her weakened physical state) "Will you come tomorrow?" I replied: "Of course, if you would like me to." She nodded. It was one of the few times she asked me to visit. I am sure she knew it was near the end.

The next day, I had just returned from taking my cat to the vet, when the phone rang. It was the nursing home telling me I should come in soon. I rang my brother and then set off immediately.

I was with her alone for a while and sang the childhood lullaby she used to sing to me when I was ill, "I Had a Little Nut Tree." My brother and I were both there when she took her last breath. A privilege, and a joyful moment, despite the sadness of the ending.

Discovering Life Coaching

While this was all happening, I had left the research company and I was working full time at the Community Health Council, but then our organisation was abolished in one of the seemingly never-ending National Health Service restructuring exercises, and we were all made redundant.

I was unsuccessful in obtaining a new full-time post but began a part-time role with a local college that drew on my experience of self-employment, helping people start their own businesses. I was the last person to leave the Community Health Council office, locking the door and dropping off the key at a nearby health service office.

That was my first experience of what we call redundancy in the UK, what other countries call 'being let go', or even 'terminated'. In theory it means your role has been made redundant, or terminated — not you personally, but it felt very painful to me.

There was a lot of support, and I received counselling during this time (and began studying a basic counselling skills course, too), but when I heard about life coaching, I decided to invest in that for myself. Very soon I realised how much I loved the process and began training to be a coach.

And so began a big, new wave that was to take me a long way. The 'wakeup call' of the cancer diagnosis had started that process, and yet coping with the treatment and the chronic pain that resulted had made it hard to stay with the lessons, and not to be swept back by the undertow as that wave ebbed. This new wave found me in a better place to ride its power.

My coach supported me while I was finding my new role with the local college. During the time I was with that organisation. I completed my coaching certificate and diploma and started my coaching practice.

As my business identity, at first I used my name, and then inspiration came from the Anais Nin (or Elizabeth Appell) quote:

> "... and then the day came when the risk to remain tight in a bud was more painful than the risk it took to blossom."

My business became Dare to Blossom Life Coaching. I developed it while working at the college part time, and finally becoming qualified as a teacher, now with adults rather than small children. I self-published my first coaching book, *Dare to Blossom: Coaching and Creativity,* in 2008.

In the years since then, I have run workshops in Cornwall, Devon, Glastonbury, Hampshire, London, and York.

Around 2012 the idea of the Dare to Blossom Rediscovery Cards emerged, and later a Companion Guide. Originally, I resisted writing the Guide as the principle was that the cards, with a single word and a colour, enabled each person to rediscover their inner wisdom. And yet people told me that a Guide with an idea of how to use them would help, so I wrote that with the intention of being just that – a guide. Not telling people what to think or how the cards should be interpreted but being a companion to stand beside them as they navigated their own way.

My contract with the local college ended in another redundancy and there were a difficult few months as I applied for dozens of positions and attended many interviews, with no success.

Finally, in August 2009, I began work as a business coach and trainer with another organisation, supporting people into starting their own business or becoming self-employed.

I loved the work, especially being out and about in the community, running group courses all over Cornwall. It was a joy to be employed to be a coach and to help people access their own inner power and potential.

I spent 12 years in that field of work and learned a lot, professionally and personally. I also experienced some big knocks to my confidence.

One event, not long after beginning work with the second organisation, truly rocked my confidence. I won't describe that in detail here, but I was removed from teaching a group with no discussion or warning. I now know that decision was not good practice in supporting teaching staff in any environment, especially those working out in the community.

In hindsight, that experience, when I felt as if I had lost touch with not only my power but also who I was – and part of that was being an experienced trainer in the subject - was the low point before another big wave rolled in to take me even higher. I did come back, home to myself, with support from many people, some at work and some in the wider community I was beginning to connect with, all over the world.

That job also ended: the vagaries of short-term project funding are brutal and, in my opinion, inefficient in resources of all sorts. The programme was eventually recommissioned, but not until a year later, and I had already decided to focus full time on my own work with Dare to Blossom.

The coaching courses I have invested in and the different professionals I have chosen to support me have taught me so much, as have the hundreds of people I have coached. I have met so many wonderful people along the way, many of them through online networking, long before I knew about Facebook. A writing group brought me a worldwide group of friends, many of whom I have now met in person.

Cat companions and spiritual guides

Throughout my life, cats have always been a constant presence for me. One of the first photos in this book shows me as a small girl with our family cat.

In the same way, so have spiritual guides always been there, although I wouldn't always have used that term, and maybe I would use other words now at times. The 'blue light' when I was a baby; the voice in the night that spoke those words: "You are safe, my child."

Maybe those insights are brought by another part of me, my higher self, my inner guidance? Perhaps, like the elements of a dream, these occurrences can be interpreted as parts of myself bringing messages?

For me, those questions are intriguing, and at the same time, not always necessary to ask. The power of the insights they bring is what is important, in the moment when it happens, and in what emerges later.

Sometimes the cat has been a spiritual guide itself. Many people who have beloved pets who leave their bodies behind feel a strong connection with them, their soul, their energy, however you may see that.

My mother was a very spiritual person. She read widely about different religions and philosophies. She believed in reincarnation and had a memory of her own of a past life. She remembered drowning, as a young woman, on a ship that sank at sea. A memory that helped her understand her fear of water. She even managed to verify it by tracking down a report of a ship that was lost at around the time and place that she perceived it to be.

She was interested in many aspects of energy: dowsing, healing, telepathy. After I left home, we didn't speak about these subjects very often, but after her stroke, when we spent a lot more time together, we shared our thoughts in some wonderful conversations.

Around the time my mother was coming to the end of her life, I was in contact with Deborah (Debbie) Clayton[ii], a clairvoyant who offered readings, describing herself as a spiritual life coach. She did these on the telephone at that time, sending a recording afterwards.

I had arranged a session for the day my mother died, which was obviously postponed. I think we spoke just a day or two later – and on that first occasion Debbie was very surprised to receive a very clear message from my mother saying all was well with her.

Apparently, she was being told she should be resting, not contacting people so soon, but she was adamant (so like her way when in life) that she had to get the message to me.

The little cat, Blackie, who I'd taken to the vet that day, my mother's 're-birthday', had to be put to sleep soon afterwards. She had an untreatable cancerous tumour on her face. She was a very friendly little cat, and when I would bring my mother for a visit from the nursing home, Blackie often came and sat on her knee whilst we were enjoying our coffee and biscuits in sunshine in the garden.

I wasn't very happy with the vet who gave Blackie the injection to put her to sleep. In my experience with many other cats for whom I have had to make this sad decision, usually they simply put it under the skin on the back of the neck. This vet was determined to get it into a vein as he said that was more humane as it worked more quickly. But he had trouble doing that, and Blackie, and I both became distressed.

Just a few days later, after receiving that message from my mother, I also was sent one by Blackie. I heard a gentle purr behind my right shoulder and felt her soft fur brush my face. I knew she too was saying: "All is well."

I have so many tales I could share of other spiritual guides and connections. At first, I needed help from other people to access the wisdom they were offering me. I had many more readings with Debbie, many more messages from my mother. Some strangely practical: one time she suggested I plant some miniature daffodils in pots outside my home office. I did that, and as I write today, in

February, they are just coming into flower yet again.

I also have two spirit guide paintings done by Patrick Gamble[iii], with a reading that takes place while he is painting. A fascinating experience on both occasions. The first time it was the face of a Chinese man who appeared on the canvas. I already 'knew' this guide through meditations. In the painting he looks very serious, I always see him as jovial and smiling. On the way home I stopped my car in a quiet spot for short while. I looked at the painting and asked the question in my head: "Why are you so serious?"

I received an immediate reply: "Of course I was being serious; it is an honour to have my portrait painted!"

The second painting, a few years later, looks uncannily like my father's father – or at least as far as we can tell from the very few old black and white photographs we have of him. The eyes in the painting look like my father's eyes. It matters little one way or the other, the connection I made was with my grandfather, who I never met. Both those paintings sit on my bookshelves, opposite the desk where I work, along with a copy of the photo of my maternal grandmother that is shared earlier in this book.

Returning to my cat companions, they have all been greatly loved and big characters, each in their own way. They often join me in my meditations, my magic carpet ride visualisation journeys. Sometimes one or other of them, sometimes a whole troupe of them, either leading or following me.

There is one particular cat I will write about here, one who was – still is – a wise old soul who has taught me some powerful lessons.

We took Sparky in after losing a previous cat who had been injured, probably by a car. Our vet had been looking after a beautiful black and white cat, he had been found as a stray and no one had come forward to claim him.

We called him Sparky as he was a 'live wire' full of energy.

Sparky soon after he arrived, July 2014

He was also extremely strong-willed and independent, and kept wandering. In hindsight, we could have guessed he would do that as he was a stray.

We took the advice to try and keep him in for two weeks. He hated it, yowling and yowling. One day he got out and disappeared, we feared we may never see him again. And yet, I thought otherwise. The next morning, a lovely summer's day when I had all the doors open, in he strolled, with a 'miaow' as if saying, "Well, where is my breakfast?" He had been and checked out his new patch and decided to stay for a while.

We live along a farm lane quite a distance from the road, but I worried about him as he kept wandering. Dave often found him some way along the road, picked him up and brought him home.

Sparky taught me so many lessons about letting go, about allowing. He had apparently had a hard life as he couldn't sit in quite a normal way as if his hips or his back legs hurt him, and the vet told us he had a heart murmur.

I love this picture of him, looking very regal ("Like Yoda," as one of my friends said) on the roof of my office, one of his favourite spots.

Sparky surveying his domain

One day he disappeared and didn't come home. After several days I began searching, putting up 'missing' posters and visiting the neighbours to ask if they had seen him. They all knew Sparky: "Oh yes, he often comes to visit, we try not to encourage him as we know he is your cat." He obviously liked to have a wide circle of friends.

About four days later, quite late in the evening, he did come home, with a badly injured back leg. We took him to the veterinary hospital, they gave him painkillers and said they would let us know the next day how he was.

When the call came, we put the phone on speaker so we could both hear: the choices were major surgery with a long recovery time when he would have to be kept indoors; or amputation of one of his back legs. As the vet said, cats adapt to that very quickly and he would be 'up and about' in no time.

We chose the second option. Later the phone rang again. Dave took the call; he didn't put it on speaker, but I could understand the message. Sparky was gone. The vet said he died when they began the anaesthesia, before the surgery began.

The physical reason may have been his heart murmur. I know he didn't wish to be a three-legged cat. He wanted to be free to roam. That night I dreamt of him: he was a shooting star whizzing off across the Universe, having fun.

He is the only one of all our cats who has chosen his own time to leave his body. We brought him home and buried him in the garden, where all our cats lie at rest.

A couple of days later I was out running a workshop. When I got home, Dave had painted the paving slab on top of his grave. He had drawn a big lightning flash (the symbol of electricians in the services, who were always known as 'sparkies'), a shooting star, and the words "On a mission. Places to go. Things to do." So perfectly epitomising this beautiful soul that had been with us for such a short time.

Since then Sparky, who I also think of as Mercury, the god of communication, whose symbol is also a lightning flash, has been with me on many meditation journeys.

Coming home to myself

The biggest wave of my life so far seems to be carrying me forward right now: connections around the world, forged through the magic of technology and supportive groups such as the Silver Tent, a community of women over 50. I joined in early 2016 when there were just a few hundred members. Today, as I write, there are well over 6000. This community, and others, has brought so many gifts of sharing and inspiration.

I also have many friends who connect in their different ways. Two women who I have known for some time now, and I form what we call a 'three-legged stool'. If one of us, one leg, wobbles a little, the other two are there to offer support on either side. We rarely see each other, but we are always connected, by text and by email, simply bearing witness for each other as we go about the daily business of living our lives. We call each other 'angel sisters' and this relationship has been such a gently powerful presence for each of us, through bereavement, job loss, moving home, new relationships, and simply the day to day ups and downs.

Since June 2015 I have returned full circle to self-employment as my only source of income, the way I started out in 1977. The power of my personal awareness and inner journeying has increased immensely in these last few years. I have built on the tools I had been developing since setting up my practice in 2003.

Beginning to speak to groups, in person and online has been a big step for this 'quiet one'. I have written more about this in the next section of this book, here is one a photo taken at one event, shortly after my 65th birthday. The title of that talk was "What's age got to do with it? Insights from a lifetime in business." I reflected on what I had learned from my mother, who was an 'entrepreneur' although she may not have seen it that way.

Plymouth Women in Business November 2017

I spoke of my experiences, from starting Pydar Crafts in 1977, through supporting many people go into self-employment in the work I did as a business coach and trainer with the two organisations, then starting Dare to Blossom Life Coaching in 2003. Finally stepping back into my own business full time in 2015.

Meditation and visualisation journeys have been a big part of my path. This one was experienced in June 2015 and will be included in my next book, *The Power of Your Compass Rose*.

This took a different 'route' to the Magic Carpet Ride Guided visualisations, with no magic carpet featuring here. Having said that, each journey is unique in any case. This experience was truly a coming home, to myself, and to all my companions along the way.

"Starting in 'reality', I am outside, on our roof terrace in the sunshine. I am surrounded by warm wood. As I enter into my meditation, I find myself walking. Walking away from a group of women, a circle. They are looking after me as I go. I hear no sounds, yet I know they are calling me back, asking me to return and re-join the circle.

I hesitate, I look at the path ahead, it looks inviting. I look back. I see the love and companionship offered there. I know I have a part to play in the circle, that without me the company of women there is incomplete. Without me the beauty of the tapestry that can be created will be missing a stitch. The power of the collaboration will be diluted.

I turn and walk back towards the waiting women. I am greeted warmly, and before I re-join the circle, two of the women lead me into one of the tents, a part of a circle of shelters that surrounds the fire pit. It is dark inside as I enter, my eyes taking a moment to adjust. Waiting to greet me is a wise elder, an older woman. She smiles, and holds up her hands, palms outwards.

Two steps…. Raising my hands, I place my palms against hers. An energy passes between us, we gaze into each other's eyes, into the windows of the soul. (In my physical 'real' world, I am placing my hands against the sun-warmed wood, this meditation has been a moving one, literally with me moving my body around, as well as emotionally.)

The wise woman embraces me warmly. As she does this, I realise that we are becoming one, we are merging ourselves, our selves, together. I have become the wise elder woman.

The two women, my two tribe sisters, lead me outside to the awaiting circle, where I take my place and we dance gently around the fire in a circle dance, sharing the warmth of our hands and the connection of our eyes and our hearts. I have come home. And I have stepped up to celebrate my years in this life and share my wisdom in a way that allows others to grow and blossom."

Rediscovering my Inner Wisdom

I believe all of my life so far has been leading me back to realising that I have the answers to my questions within me.

Since the first life coach who helped me so much, and with whom I am still in contact, I have worked with many different people as my own support team over the years. Each has provided just what I needed at that time.

Some I still work with now, either regularly or occasionally. Others I share an exchange arrangement with, where we coach each other, either within the same session, or on different days.

The process that began to emerge came from these coaching conversations, and the ideas that came from them to develop my business.

I began in June 2015, having been through that third experience of redundancy – with all that involves. The legal processes, the sadness at the ending of a successful programme. Helping to close down an office, saying goodbye to colleagues. I wanted something light and fun, and creative and inspiring at the same time.

My first idea was some 'Midsummer Magic' – an online programme and workshops – and that evolved to include a guided meditation called a 'Midsummer Magic Carpet Ride'.

This makes people smile, with a childlike delight, and the Magic Carpet Ride has been part of my 'toolbox' ever since.

That first year, I ran workshops in Cornwall, Glastonbury and London. I have expanded on my own experience and now have a process that has helped many people on their own personal journey of rediscovering their inner wisdom, reconnecting with their power within and daring to blossom.

It is now centred around the meditation poem on the next page, which I use so regularly it has become a part of me.

"Compass Rose Speaks"

By Mary Lunnen 2018

I am your Compass Rose.
My centre point is Peace. Balancing,
grounding.
Look up! Look North, to your Guiding Star.
Your Purpose.
From the East comes the rising sun.
Passion, potential.
South is the source of nature's powers.
  The flowing rivers, the rising tides, the
  ever-changing oceans.
  The wind that shapes the land. The Power
  that is arising in you.
West is the land of the setting sun.
  Progressing forwards into the night.
  Anticipating the promise of a new day.
Return your attention to your centre point,
Peace. Balanced, grounded.
I am your Compass Rose.

This combines with the Dare to Blossom
Rediscovery Cards, which have a single

word on a coloured background that can bring profound insight and with the guided visualisation of a Magic Carpet Ride, from which people bring back business ideas, career prompts, messages from those they meet.

These are used in every coaching call, every workshop, every online circle gathering. Powerful waves that have the ability to build and build.

The powerful voice of this quiet one is being heard, through interviews, podcasts, publications and the writing I do for my communities on Facebook, and elsewhere, every day.

Truly, daring to blossom is the exploration of a lifetime. I hope by sharing my journey that you who are reading these words may find some sparks of inspiration to enable you to navigate the oceans of your own life. To find and catch those powerful waves. To feel the bubbling up of joy along with your inner wisdom, and to love this wonderful life we share.

How to discover your Powerful Voice

Whether you consider yourself a 'quiet one' or not, I believe that many of us hold ourselves back from discovering our true voice, and the power it holds.

My view is that it is there, in truth to be rediscovered, as we were connected with that voice when we arrived here in this world, at the beginning of our lives.

I know I lost touch with that voice at a young age. Maybe that experience I have described, when I heard a voice speak to me as a child, was a reminder of that power. If it was, it took me many years to come back to that realisation.

So, how do we come back to that place, regain our ability to hear our inner wisdom? It may be a powerful voice once we find it, yet it often speaks very quietly. And in ways that may not seem obvious.

Do you have occasional moments of inspiration or insight? Dreams that seem of a different world than the regular 'processing' dreams that (for me at least) are mostly just a jumble? Do the words in a book, or a voice on the radio or television, sometimes seem to be talking directly to you – just to you?

I know from my coaching sessions over nearly 20 years now, since I first began working with my own life coaches, that many of these insights have come through the space and time that process offers.

The opportunity to 'hear myself think', to gain a little distance, just for a while, to allow the noisy world around me to be quietened.

Even earlier than that, I began to explore meditation, and particularly the practice of following guided visualisations. I found that worked better for me than trying to still my brain, to empty my thoughts.

Using cards of various sorts is another tool I have found productive, first the Original

Angel Cards,[iv] and then many other decks of oracle cards of various sorts. The beautiful artwork offers another dimension to the insights gained, as do the guidebooks that usually accompany them.

After a while I realised that I did not need to read that guidance, fascinating as it often was, but that I could follow the messages from my own inner wisdom. One of those messages appeared, a creative impulse, the idea of creating my own cards.

My first response was to dismiss the idea: "Who, me? Who am I to create yet another deck of cards when there are already so many?"

The reply to my question was clear and emphatic: "Who are you not to? You have been given this idea – go and bring it into reality." It can be challenging to follow that voice when it issues instructions, especially as then I had not yet truly realised it was the voice of my inner wisdom.

Have you ever had one of those 'crazy idea' moments? What did you do? Did you follow it? Or did you dismiss it? Either of those choices is right – they are simply different.

I followed mine that time, and the little cards I created have travelled out around the world, either literally, or through the photos I send to people of the cards I draw from them when we are speaking one to one or in a group.

Since I began deeply connecting again with my inner wisdom through meditation and visualisation, I have received many more insights and messages. Often, they have appeared in the form of a story, a journey, with characters using their own voices. Parts of me choosing to be represented in a dream-like scenario.

I call them 'Magic Carpet Rides' as that is the theme of the guided visualisation I use. It makes us smile and opens the way for a child like suspension of disbelief, to allow our creativity full reign to come out and play, with powerful results.

All this has been about listening to my inner voice and beginning to become clear about when what I was hearing was truly that, or something else. Often it is my inner critic I hear. That voice that says: "That is too risky. What will people think? They will laugh at you! What if you lose money? Much safer to stay where you are, keep doing what you are doing." On and on, trying to keep me 'safe'.

Safety is important of course, yet sometimes it is not what it needed. Sometimes it stifles growth. Like a plant kept in a small pot where it becomes stunted and weak, human beings need space and opportunity, to take risks within reason, to try new things, to risk failure, to dare to blossom. As counsellors often say, "If you keep on doing what you've always done, you will keep on getting what you've always got."

That brings me to the promise of this chapter: "How to discover your Powerful Voice". Choose the way that is right for you to step outside that well-known, and well-loved comfort zone. Enlist the help of friends and professionals to help, to provide support, to cheer you on, to offer a safety net.

Where do you long to be heard? At work? I know that was a key place for me. Even though in various roles I have had excellent managers who encouraged me to speak up in meetings, I often found I was simply unable to do that. Often, I did not get my thoughts organised in time to speak. Or maybe I was simply too polite and let everyone else have their say first, by which time the moment had passed.

How to tackle this? Making good notes before meetings helped. Asking to be heard before we began. If necessary, speaking to my manager after the meeting with additional thoughts. One of the things I am passionate about is how much is lost in the world of work and business when the 'quiet ones' are not heard. In a similar way to the loss of women's wisdom when they are under-represented in the workplace, there is a loss when quiet ones, whoever they, are not heard.

Is your message one you wish to spread to the wider world? I first began giving talks – something I found terrifying to start with – in connection with my passion to help women experiencing a diagnosis of cervical cancer.

For a number of years, I was invited to speak to general practice nurses who were being trained to deliver the cervical screening programme. Even though most of them were women, and they had presumably experienced undergoing the procedure themselves, many of them told me what a different perspective they gained when I shared my feelings about how I was treated – the good and the not so good.

So that can be the perfect incentive, choose something you are passionate

about, something you love talking about –
it might be a health issue, or a hobby, a
sport, a pastime - and get yourself invited
to speak about it. That passion does a lot
to overcome the nerves and the fear of
letting your voice be heard. After a while,
that power within will begin to emerge.

You may find the written word easier – as
I did at first. You can take your time; you
can revise and reconsider.

Social media has made such a big
contribution. It is simply another medium
of communication, like the book, the
newspaper, the telephone, the radio. Like
those media, it can be used for negative
or positive purposes.

For me, right from early days, I have found
it such an extraordinary way to make new
connections, to meet people around the
world I would never have encountered any
other way. Many of them I have later met
in person, and we have known that we
were already good friends.

If you truly wish to be heard in the cacophony that the internet can be, my advice – that I can only offer from my experience, that of others will be different – is to find your community first. Rather than diving in too quickly, test out different platforms and groups, find ones that feel good for you.

In recent years, I have joined business networking groups, (locally, and online), making contacts, listening to guest speakers, and learning how they worked. Later I volunteered as a speaker and have been invited to speak several times in different settings.

I have run workshops that I have organised myself for a good number of years. It was only recently that a friend pointed out that I was showing faith in myself by 'booking myself to speak' – I had not seen it that way before.

Just three years ago, I took part in my first podcast and since then have lost count of how many I have been invited to do. At first, I had to put myself forward, and still do very often, and now I also find hosts approach me.

Maybe for you, your powerful voice is not about the public sphere at all. Maybe it is within your family. For me, that can be one of the trickiest areas to navigate, and yet the one with the most gifts to offer. Learning how to calmly state what is true for you, what is important, can be the first step to negotiating a more fulfilled and happier relationship with those closest to you. Maybe not easy, but worth the effort. All these things are truly a lifetime practice – not something that is 'done' once, but rather repeated over and over, like yoga or meditation, tuning our muscles and our insight.

I return to where this section began – with you, yourself. The place where finding your powerful voice begins is within you. Truly listening to your inner guidance, what I call your "Compass Rose", your navigation system, your wisdom.

I believe that only from that point, from being truly grounded and balanced in our centre point, in peace, can we truly live the life we are here to live. Does that ring true for you?

That powerful voice of your true life expresses itself in an infinite variety of ways across our extraordinary race we call human beings.

Step into your heart, connect with your soul, and choose how to bring your one unique voice, your powerful voice into the world. Sing your song, no one else has that message, only you. If you do not, it will be lost to the world.

Start today, if not now, then when?

Postscript

Thank you for buying and reading this book. If you would like to connect with me and the work I am developing as I step more and more into my true quiet power, you will find my website and social media links in the 'About the Author' section below.

There is also a group on Facebook that you can join if you would like to join in a conversation about your own way of stepping into your powerful voice – wherever you find yourself in the infinite variety of human expression from introvert to extrovert.

My work in 2020 and onwards will be again with people around the world through the magic of technology.

I hold workshops in my beloved homeland of Cornwall, where we have the joy of meeting face to face.

Or you can choose online coaching, for individuals and with groups via videoconferencing. All utilising the powerful tools and processes I have developed over the years: the Dare to Blossom Rediscovery Cards; the Magic Carpet Ride guided visualisations; and the 'Compass Rose' which takes us from the centre point of Peace, via North, East, South and West, and returning back to the place we never left, Peace, in our centre, in our hearts.

My next publication will be the book that has been a work in progress for several years now: *The Power of Your Compass Rose,* a self-guided journey through the Compass Rose coaching process. This has proved transformational for myself and many of the people I have worked with over the last few years.

There are two extracts from that book in here, the first, in the earlier section 'Coming Home to Myself', is an example of one of my visualisation journeys. The other, found after this Postscript, is an account of a very powerful experience one day in a meditation, out on the cliff top, when I connected with my younger self at various ages. A healing journey that I know helped me to reintegrate parts of myself that had felt lost.

Since the first draft of these reflections, I have travelled around the world to New Zealand. Many people chose to join a group to journey with me in spirit on our Aotearoa Quest. It has been a deeply significant quest for me personally as I revisited that beautiful land, reconnected with my family there, and stood to speak with my own now-powerful voice on the stage at the HerStory Wellington Conference.

I leave you for now, and send deep love and gratitude to you, dear reader, and to everyone I have met along this journey. You have all given me gifts beyond description.

A Journeying Meditation on 6th October 2016

This took place on one of my favourite spots on the cliff tops near my home. Some of the birds and other creatures were there in physical reality, others simply in the spiritual realms. This was prompted by a wise healer friend, the invitation to sit in circle with all my younger selves, to gather in their strength and wisdom.

"I am straight away in the glade in the wood. I am standing by the pool, looking at the water – I am reflecting and so, literally, is the water. I invite each of my selves, each Mary from the past to join me in circle.

Mary who remembers her brother being born.

Mary who was falsely accused at school.

Mary who loved the beach and cliffs at Trevone.

Mary who lay on the thyme-scented turf on South Brent Hill.

Mary who grew into a 'flamingo' and dazzled the boys, and who survived the bullying.

Mary who went through the car crash, and who set off to university in love, and then got lost.

Mary who travelled the world and learned about men and their ways and their rough desires.

Mary who cared for her father so her mother could go to New Zealand.

Mary who was sad at the lack of understanding she had, and who loved as best she could at the time.

Mary who travelled some more, after accepting her future husband into her life.

Mary who built a business, worked hard, experienced highs and lows.

Mary who grew stronger through cancer and pain and having her womb removed.

Mary who began opening again to her higher self and eventually reconnected – "You are safe my child."

Mary the wife of over forty years, loyal if exasperated at times.

Mary the sudden stepmother and step-grandmother.

Mary the goddess standing powerful and strong.

Then – here we are, sitting in circle on the cliffs, on that gorgeous springy turf near Porthmissen Bridge. The majestic stone archways, the kittiwakes, the fulmars, the puffins, the guillemots, the kestrel, the peregrine falcon. Dolphins come close in to see us. Gannets are diving.

No one can see us, the landscape we are in is empty of other humans right now.

Just us and the animal guides. As we gather in the circle, I feel an outer ring of protection, all my guides and angels. Earth angels, sisters from other circles, and many others around the world. Keeping us safe, simply holding the circle for us to do our important work.

I breathe. I look around, then reach out my hands, to the left, to the right. I realise there is another Mary, just next to me. An energy being of Mary in the womb, who survived whatever she needed to survive before she was born. My left hand holds the hand of two and a half year old Mary and the energy being nestles between us.

About the author

Mary Lunnen lives near the dramatic coast of North Cornwall, in the far south west of the UK, with her husband and two cats. Her passion is helping people find their way home to themselves, and thus rediscover their inner wisdom. She does this through her Dare to Blossom Rediscovery Cards, a simple format with a single word and a colour, combined with her own coaching process following the points of 'The Compass Rose'. These powerful tools bring people back into conversation with their own truth, and to their centre point of deep peace

Mary draws inspiration from her love of the sea and countryside around her home, which she explores in photography and art. She began her own journey of coming home after a diagnosis of cancer in 1994 which sparked reflective journalling that grew into four published books and many articles. During 2019 she was nominated in the Lifetime Achievement category of the Venus Awards Devon and Cornwall, where she was one of three semi-finalists. She also travelled to New Zealand to speak at the HerStory Conference in Wellington.

Since 2003 Dare to Blossom Life Coaching has supported individuals and business people around the world. Mary runs inspirational workshops and on-line programmes using all the skills she has acquired and focusing around creative visualisation using the theme of a 'Magic Carpet Ride'.

Mary offers a complimentary consultation for you to find out more about how she works and decide if her approach is right for you.

To contact Mary, use one of these routes:

Website: www.daretoblossom.co.uk

Facebook business page:
www.facebook.com/daretoblossomlifecoa
ching

Readers' group: Look for 'The Powerful
Voice of the Quiet Ones' on Facebook.

Twitter: @daretoblossom

LinkedIn:
https://www.linkedin.com/in/daretobloss
om/

[i] *Positive Smear* by Susan Quilliam, 1989. Her review of my book can be found on the 'Books' page my website, here: https://daretoblossom.co.uk/about/books

[ii] https://www.deborahclayton-clairvoyant.com/

[iii] https://www.patrickgamble.co.uk

[iv] Kathy Tyler and Joy Drake

L - #0169 - 130220 - C0 - 175/108/8 - PB - DID2768378